Write an Organization History and Leave an Archive Behind

By Richard E. Mako, Jr.

Write an Organization History and Leave an Archive Behind

Copyright © 2016 by REMarkable Publications
First Edition, First Printing
10 9 8 7 6 5 4 3 2 1

ISBN-13:   978-1540483324

ISBN-10:   1540483320

Published by REMarkable Publications

REMarkable Publications, Inc.
Norwalk, Connecticut 06855

See us on Facebook:
REMarkable Publications,
Write an Organization's History and Leave an Archive Behind.

CREDITS

Edited by: Michaelann Cox

Cover Design: Richard Mako

Cover Image: Richard Mako

Printed in the United States of America

For those who anticipate the greatest future and remember the greatest past.

Richard E. Mako, Jr.
©REMarkable Publications, Inc.

<u>Contents</u>

Richard E. Mako, Jr.
©REMarkable Publications, Inc.

Acknowledgements

To Pat Kucharsky for enabling the Organization History by saving and preserving countless documents. For her patience in relaying and infusing all of the many facts and stories of our organization. Also, to Gene Kucharsky who truly modeled the life of a real writer and provided assistance and suggestion for both the history and the archive. For Senior Administrator, Dr. Arthur K. Robertson for providing the foundation and care to enable both the history and archive to become a reality.

For my wonderful wife, Michaelann, who patiently listened to my rants and raves about organization histories and organization archives and their importance in organizations, for reading the manuscript, and offering countless suggestions and interesting comments.

Introduction

Interestingly, one of my initial forays into writing an organization history

was in creating the history of a Protestant Church. I was asked by an official

committee to write the 100-year-old history, 1907 – 2007. This was a history of a

single church located in White Plains, New York: Ridgeway Christian and

Missionary Alliance Church. It was suggested to me that this should only be a

tiny pamphlet, something to hand out at a banquet that was to go along with a

series of 100 year celebratory events. The tiny pamphlet morphed into a book of

267 pages with photographs and statistical graphs, (Mako, 2010). I'm writing this to assure you that it doesn't matter what type of organization you are thinking of writing a history of as the work will be much the same.

In struggling to write this book I encountered the importance of initially creating an archive of the 100-year period. Even though I am a certified Archivist, I did not understand experientially that the way to the history was in creating the archive. Without an archive, there is no history. *So, when the history was completed I published the history and left behind an archive.* You can do the same with your organization. Write a history of your organization and leave an archive behind.

I would have certainly preferred that the archive be fully and completely established before I created the history. I could have simply, and perhaps even leisurely, poured over the archive and found my way to the 100-year history.

Instead, there was no established archive. Rather I should say an organized and orderly archive by year. What did exist were piles and stashes and more documents, photos and interviews to be conducted, and newspaper stories to read. In a real sense the archive was there, that is, it existed in however a poor state. *All* I had to do was piece it together. I note this for you versus being in a situation where few if any documents exist. For example, a fire in the past could have destroyed every paper document. There may have been an Administrative

Assistant with no vision for an archive. Instead, I could work with a wonderful and talented Administrative Assistant with a career spanning three Church Pastors. You will find yourself somewhere in between working with an already established archive to absolutely nothing documented and/or preserved. If you are serious about writing an organization history you should use whatever archive is available, and however poorly constituted, to create a better archive and thereby create the necessary documentation from which your organization history will spring.

In this book, I provide you with everything that you need to *create an organization history and leave an archive behind.*

Chapter 1 -   **How to Write an Organization History**

I share the story of how I wrote the history of an organization. It this example it was a church.

Chapter 2 -   **An Organization Archive is Important**

I share my conviction that an organization history is important and will benefit your organization.

Chapter 3 -   **How to Create an Organization Archive**

I share the story of how I wrote the organization history and Left behind an organization archive.

Richard E. Mako, Jr.
©REMarkable Publications, Inc.

Chapter 4 -   Creating a Digital Organization Archive

I share how to create a digital organization archive.

Chapter 1
How to Write an Organization History

As part of the church's 100 Year Anniversary, the chair of the committee tasked with managing 100 year festivities, approached me and asked if I would put together a history of Ridgeway Church from its beginning to the present, (1907 – 2007). I jumped at the chance to write this important document. I had three months to complete what the Chair called, "... a small pamphlet to be handed out at the banquet," (Mako, Facebook, 2016).

Richard E. Mako, Jr.
©REMarkable Publications, Inc.

I wondered, "Where should I begin?" The church was founded one-hundred years ago, (1907) but it seemed like I had a very short period of time to complete the work. Plus, a pamphlet seemed like a small undertaking for a period of one-hundred years. As I sat in my first Committee meeting, everyone agreed it was indeed time for a special anniversary celebration. They shared the goals of a special time with multiple services. Deluxe invitations with calligraphy, a banquet at the best restaurant in town, serving a sumptuous meal, were certainly appropriate. Former pastors, associate pastors, music pastors, youth pastors and administrative assistants were invited to attend and bring greetings and remember their ministry at the church, (Mako, Facebook, 2016).

Then it was time to discuss the pamphlet. The questions came very fast, from all directions.

"Do we *really* know when our church began and *who* started it?"

"Were we *always* in this building?"

"Have we saved *anything* from the past?"

"Whose job is it to save these things?"

"I'd like to get a hold of the one that chose the paneling for the sanctuary!"

"Who decided we should keep these pews. Un-padded? Give me a break!" (Mako, Facebook, 2016).

There were many more questions and several sarcastic remarks. We all shared the same basic thoughts. What *was* the history? Are there any records and if so, *where are they?* Was anybody ever *responsible* for this? I had been through this sort of thing before with other committees. Frankly, regarding the church's history, I always wondered myself how we got away with not having at least one handicapped stall in the bathrooms. One thing that everyone agreed upon- the responsibility for the history pamphlet, rested firmly on my shoulders. *Deliver 500 copies of the pamphlet so it can be given to the crowd as they streamed through the door. Expect to have 200 remaining for the future* (Mako, Facebook, 2016).

It was my responsibility to figure it all out and put together some kind of a quick organization history that could be presented to the congregation. As with most organization projects, I started with the executive in charge of the place, the Pastor and quickly made an appointment with his Administrative Assistant to see him. He had a lot of genuinely good ideas but best of all, he pointed me back to the Administrative Assistant whose career spanned three pastors or almost a third of the 100 years. She turned out to be extremely helpful. She had files and folders and secret stashes of all sorts of documents she had kept over the decades. There was the expected bank of file cabinets, and even digital folders on organization computers, which yielded plenty of information. She led me down into the basement of the organization where a large oak bookcase stood in a dark corner. I didn't even know it was there although I had passed it hundreds of times. It contained Sunday bulletin announcements stretching back decades. There were 5 year bundles of bulletins each carefully placed on the hard-light brown oak shelves. Then she led me to the church safe which I knew we used for offerings until they could be deposited in a church bank account. She turned the dial carefully, back and forth, and then swung the door open. She reached in and pulled out stacks of Annual Reports for many years, but like the bulletins, coming nowhere near the beginning decades of the church. So, between the bulletins, annual reports and, of course, the seemingly never-ending file cabinets, I had more than enough to occupy my time.

Many of the primary documents, from earlier decades, had long been lost. I guessed that many original documents might be in the homes of long-time members of the church. I issued a letter calling for all members and friends of our church to share the documents that they had and assured them that the documents would be returned and no one would blame them for keeping these records secure over the years. I received many documents from members and friends but not nearly as many as I hoped. I still believe there are many boxes of papers in attics and basements but nobody knows what they are or where they belong. Sadly, I'm sure many boxes of files and folders over the years have simply been tossed into the trash.

I began to organize the materials by year from the beginning. Some years had a lot of documents and other years almost no documents. Just when I thought I had all the available information, the Administrative Assistant, or someone from the congregation, would contact me and say they had a box of files or a bundle of photographs for me to see. In some cases, the materials were duplicates of what I had already cataloged but occasionally, someone did present me with a unique find that proved to be a significant addition. After all of this, I still had years in which there was very little information and other years with a plethora of information with copious detail. Interestingly, in some years that were bereft of information, it was not because we did not have the documents, which was certainly true for other years, but because nothing *very special* happened in that year. The church simply went about its business - worship services were conducted, Sunday school lessons taught, babies dedicated, births, deaths, visitation, and more. In these years, no new ministries were born, pastors stayed put and nothing of much value had to be replaced.

While we did benefit from having an Administrative Assistant for a few decades across the tenure of three pastors, it seemed like there was a constant flow of volunteers into and out of ministry positions. Some of this was because the church is located in a wealthy suburb of New York City which tended to

Richard E. Mako, Jr.
©REMarkable Publications, Inc.

attract men and women who either accepted a promotion and moved in or accepted a promotion elsewhere and moved out. Did a lot of documents move with them? I think so. Or, the paper was deemed redundant and trashed as an efficient part of accomplishing the move.

I organized my history by year and just kept adding details for the years. I was encouraged by some early readers to create more than simply a list of what happened. They wanted some narrative, a little commentary, observation, and some explanation, or at least a few observations. I sheepishly added what I thought was fitting and respectful and did my best to stay out of the way and provide a lattice to the dates and happenings across the hundred years. This proved to be a difficult part of writing the history. Yes, you do want to comment but not overly interpret, and certainly not splice in opinion too often. Think of the difference between a list and a good read. Make connections and provide a framework and step back and let the facts stand alone. This can be interesting because at least in years past, minutes were written with names attached to thoughts and opinions. Starting in recent years, minutes began to be washed of names, according to some, to prevent liability and opinions downplayed in the interest of unity. If I had what appeared to be the whole story it was included. If not, I relied more on simple facts and numbers. Some have reported to me that the first parts of the history are a better read, and I attribute that to more information and access to thought, explanation and opinions. I wondered exactly what should have been retained and how an ideal process would have yielded a perfect set of documents from the beginning of the organization to the present day. Sunday bulletins, Elder meeting agendas and minutes, real estate transactions all seemed appropriate and created a foundation upon which I could at least ask questions. So, do we have the bulletins? How far do they go back? Do we have Meeting Minutes for all important meetings? I was pleased to locate the mortgage and discovered that the mortgage burning service is only a *ceremony* and no one really lights the real documents on fire!

The 100th year anniversary committee imagined a thin pamphlet; a handout to the crowd attending the anniversary banquet. It seemed impossible to create a slender pamphlet for the 100 years; my digging for information clearly indicated the need for something quite a bit lager.

As I moved forward, what I found was the outline of a *rollicking* good story! Decisions were made to advance the small congregation in our local area. A story emerged of faithfulness and determination over the 100 years. Primary research information was available that provided the information needed to piece the story together. More importantly, information indicated *why* it happened and *by whom* it happened.

As my research grew, I reported back to the anniversary committee that originally convinced me to write the history. They realized right away that the pamphlet had grown to a *book sized project.* They even envisioned a *coffee table*

Richard E. Mako, Jr.
©REMarkable Publications, Inc.

sized book that they thought would be a fine work belonging in the home of every church member or church friend. Of course, I was excited and planned more chapters and dedicated myself to discovering every available document. Much did become available and I forged ahead with the now referred to *book*. There were more boxes to go through, files to secure, people to interview and photos, pamphlets and bulletins to scour. I worked part-time for more than two years to complete my work.

Beyond documents there were interviews. Who is wise and willing to discuss what happened 25, 50, 75 years ago? Which of the previous church buildings still stood? Was it still a church? Can you go and see them? Some fascinating information was unearthed by simply visiting old buildings. In my history, I discovered that the second significant organization location was previously a Jewish Social Center that included a synagogue.

The former Jewish Synagogue That Became The Church at Sterling Avenue in White Plains, New York

Photo Courtesy of The Ridgeway Church Archive

The previous tenants used oak pews that had the Star of David carved into the outside panels of each pew. There is no record of any discussion about removing the carvings or purchasing new pews or in any way ridding the pews of this symbol. Also, there were still in place large stained-glass windows depicting Old Testament stories. The records showed the church sold the building and property to The Salvation Army. Did the Salvation Army alter the pews or remove the stained glass? I telephoned them and asked about the pews and stained glass and I was told all remained as it was when purchased. Would they mind if I

Richard E. Mako, Jr.
©REMarkable Publications, Inc.

Photo by Rick Mako

photographed the windows and the pews in the sanctuary? No, they did not mind

and this led to a variety of different photos enhancing the book. (23).

Another set of photos that comes to mind is of two women driving an

automobile in the early 1900s. Apparently, the fact that they were women driving

at that time was historically important as it was not at all common for women to

drive an automobile at this time, (Tate). I used computer software to enhance

and enlarge the photo. I could clearly see what I couldn't see before. The women

were smiling broadly. In the black and white photos, you can see their beaming smiles. Why were they smiling? Another factor came to light. According to my research, one of the women in the church was the first driver in the local area to receive her drivers' license. I was unable to identify the women in the picture other than that they were associated with the church, (23). Could it be that this photo was taken in celebration of this woman receiving her license? There was no notation on the photo and no one stepped forward with information. Sadly, sometimes you can't unearth all the special information. However, at least these place marks will be fixed and at some time in the future perhaps it can be determined if this is the woman who received the first license. Her smile, as she sat behind the wheel, is included in the church history. Perhaps someday, even if she is not the first woman to obtain her license in the area, someone will be able to bear faithful witness to what her smile indicated in that automobile on that day.

Photo Courtesy of Ridgeway Archives

Greenburgh Gospel Tabernacle (1918)

Richard E. Mako, Jr.
©REMarkable Publications, Inc.

A startling fact came to light as well. In the church the Griswold family played a prominent role. Mother, father and a daughter, Caroline, attended the church. At that time, so did the founder of the church, Ms. Harriet Heyer. Mr. and Mrs. Griswold had moved to Florida to retire. They had enjoyed a prosperous business career and could invite Miss Heyer to join them in their Florida home. The Griswold's were glad to have Miss Heyer live with them but frankly Mrs. Griswold looked forward to a time when there would only be she and her husband as Harriet was quite elderly. Harriet did pass away and then within a very short few weeks so did Mrs. Griswold. Mr. Griswold decided that he would join his daughter, Caroline, in Vietnam as a missionary, which he did. Once again, the Pastor's Administrative Assistant was very helpful. She informed me that she knew Caroline and she had confided in her at this time that she was considering not returning to the Vietnam mission field and instead, fulfilling a lifelong dream of getting married. Instead, she returned to the mission field. Not long after, both Mr. Griswold and Caroline were killed by the Vietcong during the Tet Offensive in 1968 (75-76).

The idea of producing a pamphlet for the committee now seems silly with all the information that was unearthed for the book. It became a work of 267 pages of narrative, graphs and photos. Eventually the book was published. (Mako, 2010). Certainly, there is a foundation upon which the 125th Anniversary Committee can build!

Richard E. Mako, Jr.
©REMarkable Publications, Inc.

This is step-by-step list of how I created the church/organization history. Your experience will undoubtedly be different. Use this as a model for accomplishing the writing of your organization history.

1. Determine if there is an established archive. Whatever exists can be the basis of the organization's history.

   Deliverable= Assemble all known documents, graphs and photos.

2. Determine who oversees the archive. This could be an official position or simply a clerk or administrative assistant who took it upon themselves to save what they thought was important.

   Deliverable= Who is in charge past and present of the organization archive.

3. Meet with the executives and boards of the organization and explain what needs to be done to accomplish writing the history of the organization.

   Deliverable= Get on the respective meeting agendas and make your presentation.

Richard E. Mako, Jr.
©REMarkable Publications, Inc.

4. Actively assemble what is currently available of the organization history. This is anything that was saved by anyone in an official capacity. This is the active and past files of the organization.

   Deliverable= This is the organization archive.

5. Announce to the organization past and present what you are attempting to do and invite their participation. Expect that documents and photo's will be in their hands. Actively add those documents, graphs and photos that should be added to the archive.

   Deliverable= The augmented archive.

6. You will undoubtedly need to make additional pleas for documents that are missing. Add to the archive as appropriate.

   Deliverable= The augmented archive.

7. Ensure that the *Record Retention Schedule* is complete and assigned to someone moving forward. This should be an executive or administrator of the organization. This will determine what is assigned to the archive going forward.

    Deliverable= Record Retention Schedule

    Deliverable= Policy and procedure to support RRS and archive responsibility.

8. Finalize what you have and write about the organization while expecting that your work will lead to additional documents and photos presented by the organization or friends of the organization, etc.

    Deliverable= First draft of the organization history.

9. Continue writing using whatever documents are available.

    Deliverable= Additional drafts of the organization history.

10. Present a draft of the history of the organization to the executives and boards

   of the organization. This may lead to more documents and photos as

   memories are prodded.

   Deliverable= First official draft of the organization history.

11. Complete the history of the organization and present to executives and

   boards.

   Deliverable= Final presentation of the organization history.

12. Present the final version of the history of the organization to the

   executives and boards. Seek approval to release to all employees.

   Deliverable= Final and approved version of the organization history.

13. Finalize the archive of the organization which is all the documents, graphs,

   photos, et.al assembled to create the history of the organization.

   Deliverable= Present the assembled archive of the organization.

Richard E. Mako, Jr.
©REMarkable Publications, Inc.

14. Present the need of the archive of the organization to the executives and boards to ensure a continuing support of the archive.

   Deliverable= Assembled archive of the organization.

   Deliverable= Policy and procedure for support of the archive and who is now in charge of the archive.

Chapter 2

An Organization Archive is Important

In this chapter I am presenting why an archive is important and how to create an archive.

The importance of an organization archive is directly tied to the importance organization leadership associates with its long-term and short-term history. Is it important for the organization to know its *history*? Is it important for the organization to know its *beginning*? What was done to *start* the organization? How did the organization initiate departments*, recruit employees, add* buildings, develop marketing strategies, and all the many other components of an organization and its work? If you are interested in these events, or if you ever hope to be able to write your organizations' history, you should certainly consider having an organization archive. While it is obvious that those living in the future will benefit from your archive work in the present you too can benefit short-term as well. Often questions arise, especially with a new executive, answerable because you have an archive. From a basic, practical perspective, you may want to know how long a piece of expensive equipment, such as a central air conditioner or heating unit or roof, is supposed to last. When was the roof replaced? When was the air conditioner or heater replaced, and should *we* be considering a replacement? What was the original configuration of the organization offices were the offices ever remodeled? It is also about understanding. Understanding the facts as much as understanding ourselves and those who came before us, (O'Toole, Cox XVii). These questions, and other important questions, can be answered by establishing and maintaining an archive.

What is an archive?

Let's begin by defining the word archive. The formal definition comes from the archival classic, Arranging & Describing Archives & Manuscripts by Kathleen D. Roe. Roe states, "The term archives technically refers to the permanently valuable records received and accumulated by formal organizations such as governments, businesses, and non-profit organizations in the process of conducting their daily business," (1). On a more practical level, it is the central storage location of important documents including paper and photographs, which tell the story of an organization. In an organization, it tells the story of a particular organization. At this point we should also define what goes into an archive. Generally, we are concentrating on paper but an archive can certainly contain much more than paper and photographs. Furniture and other important objects may also be included in an archive. Roe has a fine list of possible inclusions to consider. "…beyond traditional paper, including moving images, audiotapes, photographs, maps, and geographic information systems, electronic record systems," (3). We may also include *digitized* documents. We remain at a crossroads in digitization with an organization or organization typically using both paper and digitized documents. (Please see Chapter 4, *Creating a Digital Archive* for more information.)

My History & Archive Experience

The idea of having an organization archive arose when I was asked to write the history of the Church/Organization. It was to be a 100-year history, 1907

Richard E. Mako, Jr.
©REMarkable Publications, Inc.

– 2007, (Mako, 2010). Absent a formal archive, I began by simply trying to locate important documents from the past. I discovered that the Administrative Assistant to the Pastor had served not only the current pastor but 2 previous pastors. Her service totaled more than 35 years. She was a professional, detailed oriented and retained many different documents and faithfully maintained these documents in a variety of different locations in the organization. There was no established archive but her retention of key documents was not only good news it was a good *start* in writing the history. Of course, my work would have undoubtedly been much simpler and faster if there was an official archive, but the current situation was far better than I had hoped, and much better than another writer might be confronted with in writing the history of their organization. Fortunately for me, the Administrative Assistant had the foresight to maintain an informal archive. She said no one asked her to do it. She simply saw it as a prudent thing to do. Absent a complete and maintained archive, a knowledgeable Administrative Assistant, with decades of experience, is a great resource. Without the benefit of an Administrative Assistant, or other person with this kind of foresight, the job of creating a history and establishing an archive will be exponentially more difficult. Sadly, it may be actually impossible to assemble much of any kind of archive at all. Even with the help of this outstanding person, as I did my research, I did not find the needed documents in a single place or even in 10 locations. Much depended upon the memory of the Administrative Assistant. I asked for the documents and she did her best to supply them. Some were initially denied as non-existent but later a location resulted from a burst of her memory. We went upstairs and we went downstairs. We went behind, between and beneath. There were large stock piles of documents that were all but worthless and short stacks of documents that were invaluable. Just as I began to think I have come to the end of the history based on all available documents, suddenly she would present me with a cachet that was integral to writing the history. Some documents she thought were routine, and not very important, were vital such as the organization bulletin. Often, she simply forgot about where she had stashed certain documents such as the annual reports which she had faithfully salted away for decades in the Treasurer's safe. Without her I do believe I would have said the organization history was all but impossible to piece together.

I extended my reach for documents by issuing a letter to members and friends of the organization, past and present, local and faraway, explaining what I was doing and asking for documents and photos. Many answered the letter and followed up with many important documents and photos, but many more boxes and trunks are full but sitting in a garage or an attic. In some cases, no one knows they are there. I wrote the 100-year history over a two-year period. Initially, the Committee envisioned a small pamphlet to be handed out at the 100-year banquet. Instead the pamphlet morphed into a 267-page book filled with photos.

What is in Place?

My experience in writing our organization history highlights some of the most important aspects of establishing an organization archive. Of course, you want as much of a good foundation in place as possible. Be thankful if there is any foundation at all in place. Ask the following questions-

First, is there an archive (however limited) already in place? Does it represent the historical period of interest? In my experience, I was interested in a period of 100 years. However, absent the full 100 years, I was certainly interested in any good information within that 100-year time period. On a practical level, find out what is available. In most situations, *someone* at *some time* will have *saved something*. Hopefully it is a complete history but often it will not be. You may have had a sympathetic Administrator and/or Administrative Assistant for a period and then no one supporting the archive for another extended period. You should deal with what you have and try to make it better.

Second, is someone in charge of the archive in an official or, in my experience, unofficial way? I had a dedicated Administrative Assistant with documentation and personal experience for almost half of the history years. But what about the other years? Ideally, your history should have some sort of archive and contact with however many people that were involved over the historical years in question. Having a successful transition from decade to decade is naturally *the* goal. Sadly, there was no other person like the Administrative Assistant in the past although many did participate, and some were quite helpful. Who are the people that were in charge or at least close to retaining records and maintaining an archive? There should be a current person, such as a secretary or administrative assistant or even organization administrator responsible for an archive or, at least, close to these areas. Seek them out and trace back as far as you can go. Interestingly, there was more solid information available in the distant past than in the recent past and near present day. You may have to find people who are retired or who have moved away and interview them. Naturally, you should meet and build relationships with people that are either newly retired or who currently work in the organization.

Third, you should deal creatively with whatever situation presents itself regarding the remaining years and discover the necessary documentation. I was thrilled to have 40 years of good documentation but still had to confront the remaining 60 years and develop a plan to discover those documents. I could have faced, and you may face, 100 years of little documentation and no clear path towards discovery of the rest. One person may bring you to the proverbial dusty trunk in the attic where you will discover stacks of every desirable document waiting and neatly rubber-banded. Or, not. You will have to respond to whatever situation is presented. You may have nothing or much of anything along the way to a wonderful and intelligent record retention system and a fully

Richard E. Mako, Jr.
©REMarkable Publications, Inc.

conceived and maintained archive.

Fourth, you must continually focus on only important documents. You may find plenty of the wrong documents and little if any of the important documents. Be relentless, but be thankful for what was retained and maintained. Stacks of worthless documents may indicate the possibility of stacks of valuable documents.   Do these documents represent important milestones in the organization? Do the documents represent what took place in the 100 years of the organization? Remember to be selective. There is such a thing as very old, perfectly preserved, but worthless document that should have been trashed decades ago, but for some reason was retained. Naturally, the reverse is true as well. You may find a very old, tattered document stuffed behind the file drawer that is a priceless artifact of your organization's history. Roe said succinctly, "Simply having something ""old"" does not make it archival-and something quite new can definitely be archival because it provides evidence of a person or organization's activities," (29). Create standards for record retention and archiving with organization leaders and stand by those standards.

Fifth, is there a Record Retention policy and procedure in place with a record retention schedule? Even better if it has been used for many decades! Start by ensuring that an intelligent record retention policy and procedure along with a record retention schedule are in place. This is the foundation of a great archive.

Richard E. Mako, Jr.
©REMarkable Publications, Inc.

Following these foundational recommendations will move you well on your way to establishing your organization archive.

Record Retention

A Record Retention policy and procedure must be in place for a fully functioning archive to thrive. Of course, you would prefer that it was in place during the entire history of your organization. In many situations you will find a portion of a record retention policy and procedure. There will be something in this space but it will most likely have to be dramatically improved. In fact, Boles says, "Archivists should engage records creators and record users in a continuous discussion about the nature of what the archival record should be," (22). The purpose of Record Retention is to do just that – retain records. Think of it as a precursor to an archive. An organization has a variety of documents that *define* it as an organization. Some typical documents are the following:

- Agendas

- Meeting Minutes

- Annual Reports

- Quarterly Reports

- Offering Reports

- Strategic Reports

- Requisitions

- Purchase orders

- Shipping Manifests

- Tax Returns

- Selected correspondence

Richard E. Mako, Jr.
©REMarkable Publications, Inc.

Record Retention Schedule

Next, you will need to create the record retention *schedule*. Boles defines the Schedule as, "…the various types of records found within an agency, specifies how long those records will remain in active storage within the creating agency's own electronic or paper files, determines when the records will be transferred to a ""records center"" or taken off-line, and determines the records' final disposition at the end of their inactive phase," (54). A RRS is your list of documents identified by the management of an organization (Executives, Managers, Supervisors, staff, et.al.) that evaluates the work of the organization and indicates which documents are important, and for how many weeks/months/years those documents should be retained before going into the archive. Keep in mind too that not every document will be retained and many will simply move to the trash. Likewise, many documents will be retained for long periods of time but ultimately not move to the Archive. Imagine the cost of retaining and maintaining documents. Imagine all the wasted hours chasing after these documents and trying to ensure they are where they need to be when needed.

The schedule should look like this.

Document #	Title	Responsible	Time	Responsible	Deposit
12345	Vice-President Meeting Agenda	VP	Retain for 24 months and move 12 months to Archive annually.	VP	Archive
678910	Senior VP Staff Meeting	SVP	Retain for 24 months and move 12 months to Archive annually.	SVP	Archive
111213	Weekly Department Meetings	CEO	Retain for 24 months and move 12 months to Archive annually.	CEO	Archive

Document #

Each document should be assigned an identifying number (number and letters is fine).

Title

Official title of the document.

Richard E. Mako, Jr.
©REMarkable Publications, Inc.

Responsible

Who is the creator of the document or primary user of the document?

Time

How many *months* should this document be retained once it is complete? Complete equals the useful life of the document. It may be when the document is filled out or when the report is final.

Responsible

At the end of the document's life who is responsible for making the decision to move or not move to the archive?

Deposit

The responsible person that assigns the document to the archive should also determine how many months it should remain in the archive before it is reviewed again. The alternative is the document is destroyed or trashed.

Each created document should be on the RRS. New documents should be placed on the RRS and assigned a retention and older documents should be reviewed and as necessary, their retention schedule adjusted. In general, a organization should purposely create documents and then carefully determine how long each should be retained. You will have documents that have a retention set by Federal or State law. For example, the *I-9 Employment Eligibility*

Verification form must be retained for a minimum of 3 years or 1 year more than the employee's termination date, (U.S. Citizenship and Immigration Services 37). Each assigned retention date should be carefully considered and assigned. You should also appreciate that this schedule will generate a nearly continuous flow of documents from immediate use to storage, when appropriate - trash and, possibly, to the archive. Consider requirements not only for handling but also space. You will also need to include responsibility for all of this on multiple job descriptions. You will also have to carefully consider allocating space not only for initial retention but for storage and then for the archive. Obviously your archive can only be as good as your RRS.

RRS To Archive

Naturally, the decision to retain a document should be because the document is *vital* to understanding what the organization or organization is all about. Ask yourself if the document gives the reader a view toward understanding the organization. Not every record retained on the RRS should be automatically retained in the archive. And, not every document, even if it is maintained for a long period, belongs *automatically* in the archive. Be persnickety about which documents move to the archive. Boles adds, "For most records the final decision will be destruction. Only a small proportion of all documentation finds its way into an archive," (54). Remember to add a retention time for the archive as well. Certainly, not every document in the archive has to have an indefinite time period extending forever into the future. Finally, you may also want to actively identify records as candidates for retention and archival early in the process. Roe thinks this is important, saying,

> "Records with archival value need to be identified early in their life cycle. Organizations with competent records-management programs ensure records are managed in a way that supports the identification of permanently valuable groups of records and that necessary information about the creation and use of the records survives for use by the archives," (8).

How It All Can Work

You know you have a year's worth of *VP Agendas*. They are fine where they are currently located. Now you have 10 and then 15 years' worth and they occupy a couple of file cabinets. They are valuable and you have 2 copies of each Agenda. After 10 years, 5 years should be placed in the official organization archive. This means that at any given time the organization has an active file of at least 5 years of Agendas for historical research and in the sixth year moves the sixth oldest year of Agendas to the archive. It also means that you may schedule this move as convenience, space and, of course, any special preservation concern, allows. You have identified other documents that should be retained including *VP Meeting Agendas* and *SVP Meeting Minutes*. The Agendas tend to be no larger than one-half page and the Meeting Minutes come in at about 2 pages. These documents are identified for the archive and will be retained for five years and each year the latest (6th) year will move to the archive. The same will be done for other important documents. This continues with an evaluation of all of the documents produced by the organization in its day-to-day activities. This is about *management* and not allowing every piece of paper to be kept on into the future with more and more file cabinets purchased every year. While it may seem like a tragedy for documents to be trashed and not enter the archive it is equally sad to simply save every document and not be *selective* at all. The decision to save, for how long, and whether to save additionally in the archive, is a decision that requires thought and calculation.

From my perspective as historian, I was glad documents were retained – all documents. But from a practical standpoint, as well as an archival perspective, ideally you want the decision-maker to make a careful and calculated decision. If the record retention and archive decision-making tends to be too liberal, you will retain too many documents and/or for too long a period and too many hours will be spent in retaining and archiving endeavors. If the decision-making tends to be too conservative, you will retain too few of the important documents. Balance will reinvigorate the integrity of both the RRS and the Archive.

The 100-year celebration came and went and I was given a reprieve because I was now working on a history book versus a pamphlet. The book came in at 267 pages with historical photographs and committee members, as well as the purchasers of the book, were pleased. An additional benefit to doing the book was the establishment of an official organization archive to be maintained by the Organization Administrator. Finally, I highly recommend considering the status of your organization's RRS and Archive. You can start very small and identify a few documents that require retention and later archiving. Find a sturdy file cabinet and build from there. Make sure all key managers are on board and backing the processes. Someone should be tasked with responsibility for the RRS and the Schedule. Each time a new form is created the person or group tasked with responsibility for records should be involved in a discussion about the associated retention time and archive possibilities. Decisions around retaining and archiving documents should become a natural part of administrative flow.

Once your record retention system is in place, including an updated record retention schedule, employees should include record retention and archive recommendations whenever new forms or documents are created. At our organization, the Organization Administrator was assigned to manage record retention, create the record retention schedule and the new archive. In fact, she recently recommended changing the retention on several documents and moving another document into the archive for longer retention. Her next goals include moving forward on purchasing a de-humidifier to regulate temperature.

Richard E. Mako, Jr.
©REMarkable Publications, Inc.

Chapter 3
How To Create an Organization Archive

This chapter is dedicated to assisting you in creating an organization

archive. While I am a certified Archivist, I did not appreciate the true and practical

value of an archive until I wrote a history for my organization/church titled,

Ridgeway 1907 – 2007 A History of The Christian and Missionary Alliance

Organization of White Plains, (Mako, 2010). How do you write a history of your organization without an archive? What do you do when many years of history are not adequately represented by organization documents? When confronted with these questions you can imagine you begin to see the value of an organization archive as well as its precursor, the Record Retention Schedule.

At this point, you should understand the importance of an organization archive and be convinced that your organization should have an archive. You may want to consult my article titled, *The Importance of Having an Organization Archive*, (Mako, 2016) if you have not reached this important point. This article will directly address how to move forward and create a organization archive.

You may be an executive or a manager, or simply a concerned organization member who has come to the conclusion that a organization archive is important and your organization should have one. At this point you are wondering how to go create the archive. Establishing an organization archive is not difficult but it is challenging. You will have passed the most difficult hurdle when you convince your manager or executive that one is important and needed. If you are the executive or manager, create a proposal and place it on the next board agenda. Ask for an appointment with your manager/supervisor and plead your case. Write up a proposal and show benefits and costs. Let's assume you have gained approval and you are either the sole project manager or you are working on a team to make the archive happen. What do you do next?

Record Retention

Record retention is not the organization archive but it is a necessary first step toward establishing a organization archive. You will need to establish a record retention program at your organization prior to establishing an archive. You will need to take a look at the records generated by your organization and work with respective managers to determine which records are worth saving. Are any documents saved at all? While certainly much can be said about a digital archive, in most situations you will be chasing paper documents. By all means move to establishing a digital archive but that discussion is for Chapter 4. In record retention you are considering records from a practical standpoint as well as from an historical standpoint. Some records will have to be retained simply because federal or your state law says it must be. For example, the *I-9 Employment Eligibility Verification* form must be retained for a minimum of 3 years or 1 year more than the employee's termination date, (U.S. Citizenship and Immigration Services 37). Each assigned retention date should be carefully considered and assigned.

A Record Retention Schedule should look something like this.

Record Retention Schedule

Form	Number	Owner	Responsibility	Retention	Ending	Deposit	Duration	Special Instructions

Form

Description of form called Elder Meeting Agenda

Number

Assigned number of form

Owner

Who is responsible for placing form in file and retaining form.

Responsibility

The person responsible for ensuring that this form is retained.

Retention

The duration of retention.

Ending

When the form can be moved.

Deposit

What is the decision for this form? Can it be destroyed or should it move to the organization archive?

Duration

How long will the item be retained in the organization archive?

Special Instruction

Are there any special instructions regarding this item while it is stored in the archive?

Naturally, the organization will have all sorts of forms and other paper documents that it retains as a routine part of its Record Retention Schedule. You should track down each form and identify its associated information. Place this vital information on the Record Retention Schedule. Enlist anyone that is involved in generating, maintaining or disposing of forms. Some will be easy to locate. Most organization units meet periodically and produce an agenda and meeting minutes. Decide whether these documents should be retained. Every organization unit will have to be evaluated and a decision made about the produced documents and forms. Some agendas and meeting minutes will be saved, and others trashed. In most cases agendas and meeting minutes will be

saved, but after being retained even for a long period of time, eventually trashed

and not archived.

Here is an example of a completed Record Retention Schedule.

Form	Number	Owner	Responsibility	Retention	Ending	Deposit	Duration	Special Instructions
VP Meeting Agenda	101	SVP	SVP – Administrative Assistant	36 months	72 months	Archive	Indefinite	Archive Control General
SVP Meeting Agenda	102	CEO	CEO – Administrative Assistant	36 months	72 months	Archive	Indefinite	Archive Control General

The schedule is added to as executives, managers and supervisors

identify more important documents. Be sure to account for all documents. Some

will have no retention period or a very short retention period. Some will reach the

archive and have an assigned period in the archive and others will be initially

retained and then move to the trash never seeing the archive. Organization

policy and procedure documentation should support the idea and importance of

the archive as well as record retention and the record retention schedule.

You should also consider the *movement* of documents so you build in efficiency. In the SVP Meeting Agenda, Form 102, owned by the CEO with responsibility assigned to the Administrative Assistant, the AA assigned 36 months' retention or 3 years. The time is then *doubled* to ensure that there is always at least three years available in the regular retained files and at least three years is *moved* to the archive. The initial three-year period affords the organization time to consult the form, use it in reports, etc. Considering the need for doubling, you may want to limit the Agendas to 1 year in the office at any given time and transfer the remaining documents to the archive. This will result in more flexibility. In this example you need only ensure that 1 year of documents is present in the office file and move the documents realistically after two years.

All RRS decisions should be made carefully as retention translates into cost such as manpower, folders, file cabinets, transfer to archive, etc. As many bad decisions to throwaway valuable documents that should have been retained, have been made, as have been made to retain documents that should have been tossed.

What About The Past?

Most organizations start off with a RRS that deals with the present and a certain number of documents dictated more by readily available file space than by careful decision making. This means you have the present to address and whatever is in the files and, of course, what is missing. You may be in luck and files were available as the years progressed. Almost certainly, unless your organization is quite young, you will be missing years of documents from the distant past. First, ensure that the present is addressed and results in an up-to-date RRS and you have in place policies and procedures that govern creation of documents, management of what is filed and how documents move to and are managed in the new archive. Next, address the past by sending out a letter or e-mail that explains what you are doing and asks for documents that fill-in the missing documents from the past.

Archive

Once documents are moving from regular files to the organization archive the documents must be preserved and made available to those that need to review them. The number of months assigned to remain in the operating file prior to moving to the archive should be set at a high enough level so that the archive is not serving an excessive number of document requests. It may take you time to reach a sensible balance.

Promoting The Archive

It is very important to ensure that you write a periodical report to ensure that everyone knows the significant value of the archive to the organization. Track your documents from start to their eventual use in the archive. Tell the stories you hear about the benefits accruing to your organization because you have archived documents. Even if you are not asked to do so, I recommend you write a short history of your organization that uses archived documents. Perhaps a pamphlet in this case will be enough. When new executives, managers or supervisors arrive provide them with historical information about the organization. When questions arise and no one seems to have an answer, search the archive and, if possible, provide the answer. Here is an example of the questions I was asked when I wrote the 100-year history of my organization.

"Do we *really* know when our organization began and *who* started it?"

"Were we *always* in this building?"

"Have we saved *anything* from the past?"

"Whose job is it to save these things?"

"I'd like to get a hold of the one that chose the paneling for the lobby!"

(Mako, 2015).

Encourage SVPs, VPs, Board members, Supervisors, Managers, and others to use and contribute to the archive. Make periodic presentations to departments and other units to introduce the archive and then to make status and highlight updates. As you do this, organization leadership will grow to appreciate the archive and its many benefits to the organization.

Responsibility and the Archive

You may have had great success in getting the archive going as well as initiating record retention and the record retention schedule but eventually someone must maintain it all. Who is going to do that? There are many possible alternatives for this position. Your best strategy is to fold responsibility into an Organization Administrator or an Office Services Department job description. Remember the benefit I received in writing the Organization History by having an Organization Secretary/Administrative Assistant with a heart for the history of my organization. This person may exist to help you in the initial steps of creating an archive and may exist to assist and possibly manage the archive going forward.

Richard E. Mako, Jr.
©REMarkable Publications, Inc.

Chapter 4
Creating a Digital Organization Archive

For many of you the digital archive seems like a daunting task. Of course,

you should have in place the paper archive before tackling the digital archive.

However, you will find that the principles underlying creating the paper archive

will be the same as creating the digital archive.

Richard E. Mako, Jr.
©REMarkable Publications, Inc.

As a society we have discussed the so-called inevitable demise of paper for decades. Instead, paper has grown in use and will continue to grow in use. Statista, a leading business statistics website sees at least 1% growth through 2020, (Statista). At the same time, *born as digitized documents* are added in great numbers every day. According to Statista, digital documents are, "…doubling in size in every two years, and by 2020 the digital universe – the data we create and copy annually – will reach 44 zettabytes, or 44 trillion gigabytes,…" (EMC2).

So, while paper remains an important archival item, digital documents are advancing at even a higher rate.

From an archival theory perspective, there are few differences between the paper archive and the digital archive. You should go through all the same steps to achieve a digital archive that you did to establish the paper archive. This chapter addresses only the creation of the digital archive with associated digital record retention policy and procedure, including digital documents on the Record Retention Schedule. Obviously, there are operational differences in handling a digital archive versus handling a paper archive. Let's start with the fact that paper is tangible and will need to move physically through the various stages from operational use to the archive while a digital document will move exclusively within electronic files from the operational file to the archival file.

Richard E. Mako, Jr.
©REMarkable Publications, Inc.

At this point, you should understand the importance of both paper as well as digital organization archives and be convinced that your organization should have both a paper and a digital archive. You may want to review foundational archive concepts through my experience in writing the 100 year organization history in my Book titled, "Ridgeway 1907 – 2007 A History of The Christian and Missionary Alliance Organization of White Plains," (Mako, 2010), or in articles, "The Story of Writing the Organization History," and "The Importance of Having an Organization Archive" (Mako, 2015). You are now ready to move forward in creating a digital archive for your organization.

You may be a VP, SVP or a Supervisor or Manager. Work within your chain of command and develop an appropriate proposal. At this point, you are wondering how to create the digital archive. Like an initial paper archive, creating a digital organization archive is not *difficult* but it is *challenging*. You will have passed the most difficult hurdle when you convince your VP or SVP that the digital archive is important and needed. If you are a Supervisor or Manager create a proposal and place it on the next VP/SVP agenda. Write up a proposal and show benefits and costs. Your supervisor may be lower in rank to VPs or SVPs but you can still create a convincing proposal and convey the importance of a digital archive.

Remember, your organization has already created a paper archive, so a digital archive is an extension of that important work. Just as your organization

Richard E. Mako, Jr.
©REMarkable Publications, Inc.

leadership became convinced of the need and importance of the paper archive, they should see the wisdom in creating the digital archive.

Let's assume you have gained approval and you are either the sole project manager or you are working on a team to make the archive happen. What do you do next?

Information Technology & Your Organization

Unlike the paper archive, in which paper may be all over the physical plant of the organization, digital documents are typically located in a single place – your organization's computer system. It is also possible that your organization is small and has desktop computers that are stand-alone and not networked. Or you may have a small network of computers. If that is the case, you should interact with each computer as a stand-alone computer and see what is being stored on each computer. It is also possible that older digital documents have been backed-up to a remote server. Your goal is to account for all born digital documents.

Your job is easier if there was a hard transition from paper to digital. In most cases, moving from paper to digital was a gradual move that continues to the present, with some documents born paper and some born digital. An associated benefit to this work is to identify documents that are redundant, i.e. multiple copies of the same document in different media, that is, paper and

Richard E. Mako, Jr.
©REMarkable Publications, Inc.

digital. This may also extend to multiple copies of each media and more.

It is vital that you identify the people who serve your organization in *information technology*. Depending on the size of your organization, you will either have one or more information technology professionals on your payroll. Your organization may also have a relationship with one or more computer vendors that service your stand-alone computers or network of computers. You will need to understand their role too. Further, you will need to account for all people that create and/or modify digital documents. This is not any different than identifying all the people that create and/or modify paper documents. Your information technology representatives should be able to provide you with all of the information you need. In fact, they may have already created a form of an archive that will provide you with a good start.

You will also need to seek out a person or persons that create the policy and procedure on document creation. Is there an organized way to track form creation with numbers and letters, i.e. F1, F2, F3 with F standing for form. Again, this may exist for paper documents and not for digital documents. It is imperative that you add digital documents to these policies and procedures.

Record Retention

Does anyone already do record retention, and is there a Record Retention Schedule? Remember, all of this should be in place if there is a paper archive. If it is not in place, or it is partially in place, it must be created before a viable digital archive can be initiated. We are basically moving forward under the impression that a paper archive with record retention and a Record Retention Schedule is already in place.

You will also need to lead the charge to moving to digital documents from paper. Initially, your Record Retention Schedule will undoubtedly have paper and digital documents. There may be a reason for having documents in both paper and digital and, of course, there will be older documents exclusively in paper. A project for later will be to move paper documents exclusively to a digital format. At this point, ensure that all documents, whether paper or digital are appropriately represented in the Record Retention Schedule.

A Digital Record Retention Schedule should look like this.

Form	Number	Owner	Responsibility	Retention & Address	Ending	Deposit & Address	Duration	Special Instructions
VP Meeting Agenda	101	SVP	Administrative Assistant	36 months	72 months	Archive VP Meeting Agenda. Meeting Agendas Dates	Review after 5 years.	Digital

Form

Description of form called VP Meeting Agenda

Number

Assigned number of form

Owner

Who is responsible for placing form in file and retaining form.

Responsibility

The person responsible for ensuring that this form is retained.

Richard E. Mako, Jr.
©REMarkable Publications, Inc.

Retention & Address

The duration of retention & Digital address.

Ending

When the form can be moved.

Deposit Address

What is the decision for this form? Can it be destroyed or should it move to the organization archive? Also, digital address.

Duration

How long will the item be retained in the organization archive? In examples, review after 5 years.

Special Instructions

Indicate whether paper or digital.

Richard E. Mako, Jr.
©REMarkable Publications, Inc.

Here is an example of a completed Digital Record Retention Schedule.

Form	Number	Owner	Responsibility	Retention & Address	Ending	Deposit & Address	Duration	Special Instructions
VP Meeting Agenda	101	SVP	Administrative Assistant - SVP	36 months VP	72 months	Archive Meeting Agendas, Board.Meeting Agendas Dates	Review after 5 years.	Digital
SVP Meeting Agenda	102	Administration Board	Organization Administrator	36 months	72 months	Archive	Review after 5 years.	Digital

The schedule is added to as executives/managers/supervisors identify additional important digital documents. Be sure to account for all digital documents. Some will have no retention period or a very short retention period. Some will reach the archive and have an assigned period of time in the archive and others will be initially retained and then move to the trash never seeing the archive. Organization policy and procedure documentation should support the idea and importance of the archive as well as record retention and the record retention schedule.

You should also consider the *movement* of documents so you build in efficiency. In the Administration Meeting Agenda, Form 102, owned by the Administration Board with responsibility assigned to the Organization Administrator, the Organization Administrator assigned 36 months' retention or 3 years. The time is then *doubled* to ensure that there is always at least three years available in the regular retained files and at least three years is *moved* to the archive. The initial three-year period affords the organization time to consult the form, use it in reports, etc. Considering the need for doubling, you may want to limit the Agendas to 1 year in the office at any given time and transfer the remaining documents to the archive. This will result in more flexibility. In this example, you need only ensure that 1 year of documents is present in the office file and move the documents realistically after two years.

All RRS decisions should be made carefully as retention translates into cost such as hours, folders, file cabinets, transfer to archive, etc. As many bad decisions to throwaway valuable documents that should have been retained, have been made, as have been made to retain documents that should have been moved to trash.

What About The Past?

Most organizations start off with a RRS that deals with the present and a certain amount of documents dictated more by what is in digital folders than by careful decision making. This means you have the present to address and whatever is in the folders and, of course, what is missing. The cost of digital space has dropped over the years so it is likely that there are many years' worth of paper and digital documents available. Some of these files and their folders may be in back-up mode, that is, located in a different location than the more recent operating files and folders. Naturally, an ideal scenario is that all paper and all digital documentation is available. It is likely because of the low cost that all or at least a significant portion of digital documents are available either in operating folders or in backup folders.

Once digital documents are moving from operations files to the organization digital archive the digital documents must be preserved and made available to those that need to review them. The number of months assigned to remain in the operating file prior to moving to the archive should be set at a high enough level so that the archive is not serving an excessive number of digital document requests. It may take you time to reach a sensible balance.

Richard E. Mako, Jr.
©REMarkable Publications, Inc.

Promoting The Digital Archive

It is very important to ensure that you write a periodical report to ensure that everyone knows the significant value of the digital archive to the organization. Track your digital documents from start to their eventual use in the digital archive. Tell the stories you hear about the benefits accruing to your organization because you have archived digital documents. Even if you are not asked to do so, I recommend you write a short history of your organization that uses archived digital documents. Perhaps a pamphlet in this case will be enough. When a new executive/manager/supervisor arrives provide her with historical information about the organization. When questions arise and no one seems to have an answer, search the archive and, if possible, provide the answer.

Encourage managers, VPs, SVPs and others, to use the digital archive. Make periodic presentations to organization boards and the congregation first to introduce the digital archive and then to make status and highlight updates. As you do this, organization leadership and the congregation will grow to appreciate the digital archive and its many benefits to the organization.

Responsibility and the Archive

You may have had great success in getting the digital archive going as well as initiating digital record retention and the digital record retention schedule but eventually someone must maintain it all. Who is going to do that? There are many possible alternatives for this position. Your best strategy is to fold

Richard E. Mako, Jr.
©REMarkable Publications, Inc.

responsibility into an Organization Administrator or VP/SVP's job description.

Including digitized documents in your organization's archive will be a significant plus to your organization. Your best strategy is to work with the people that are already diligently working on the current, mostly paper archive. Work with your information technology people and with those who write policy and procedure and ensure that the Record Retention Schedule is modified to include digital documents. Promote the new digital documents to your organization. Do your best to help in the transition from just paper to born digital documents. Your organization will benefit by this addition to the archive!

Richard E. Mako, Jr.
©REMarkable Publications, Inc.

Works Cited

Boles, Frank. Selecting & Appraising Archives & Manuscripts. Chicago: Society

    of American Archivists, 2005.

Mako, Richard E. Ridgeway 1907 – 2007: A History of the Christian and

    Missionary Alliance Organization of White Plains. Createspace, 2010,

    New York.

Mako, Richard E. The Importance of Having an Organization Archive: Facebook.

    September 30, 2016. [November 15, 2016. https:///www.facebook.com

    /Ridgeway–100year–History–of–the–CM–Achurch–in–white–plains-

    24251135416/.]

Mako, Richard E. The Story of Writing the Organization History: Facebook.

    October 30, 2016. {November 15, 2016. https:///www.facebook.com

    /Ridgeway–100year–History–of–the–CM–Achurch–in–white–plains-

    24251135416/.]

N.a. EMC2 Digital Universe with Research & Analysis by IDC. IDC. EMC2.

    Web.5 August 2915.

N.a. Statistics and Facts About The Global Paper Industry. Statista. Statista,

    Inc. Web.15 August 2015.

O'Toole, James M., Cox, Richard J. Understanding Archives & Manuscripts.

    Chicago: Society of American Archivists, 2006.

Roe, Kathleen D. Arranging & Describing Archives & Manuscripts. Chicago:

    Society of American Archivists, 2006.

Tate, Robert. The Early Days of Women Automobile Drivers. Motorcities

National Heritage Area-Story of The Week. Motorcities.Org. 21 July 2013.

Web. 18 May 2016.

U.S. Citizenship and Immigration Services. Handbook for Completing Form I-9

(Employment Eligibility Verification Form) Publication No. M-274 (Rev.

04/03/07), U.S. Government Printing Office. 2007, Washington, DC.

Index

Richard E. Mako, Jr.
©REMarkable Publications, Inc.

Biography

Richard E. Mako, Jr. has been involved in evaluating organizations from many different perspectives in multiple industries for decades. He began as an Evaluator for the United States General Accounting Office in Los Angeles, California. He completed a Bachelor of Arts degree in Political Science with an emphasis in City Management at California State University, Los Angeles. He moved to the Center for Public Resources also in Los Angeles. The CPR is an umbrella organization that functions like a government incubator for fledgling organizations like the California Association of Public Information Officers (CAPIO) and the Southern California Labor Relations Council (SCLRC.) At the CPR, where he rose to become Interim Executive Director, and working for the SCLRC, Mr. Mako led efforts to establish a neutral total compensation database to provide data for negotiating state and local government worker contracts. He also coordinated the League of California Cities Total Compensation Salary Survey for Los Angeles and Orange Counties. While at the CPR, he served with the Urban Institute on its study, *Performance Measurement in Local Governments*. Richard became Assistant to the City Manager of Alhambra, California where he coordinated the Human Resources office, researched and developed policy and implemented Human Resources and associated projects. Later, he moved to the private sector, accepting the position of Organization and Compensation Analyst, for Home Savings of America where he was responsible for designing and implementing organization and compensation policy and plans. California Federal Bank recruited him for his systems and organization background where he rose to Vice-President of General Services. Richard added degrees in Multimedia and Technology as well as in one of his passions, a Master of Arts in Writing. Richard became a certified Project Manager with the Project Management Institute and has managed many projects with an Information Technology emphasis for automotive, multimedia and consulting companies.

Richard lives with his wife Michaelann and their Welsh Pembroke Corgis, Eddie and Bogie, in southern Connecticut.

Mr. Mako's Other Publications

Mako, Richard E. *Compensation Planning for Churches: How to Pay Your Pastor and Every Other Church Worker,* Createspace, 2016. Print.

Mako, Richard E. *Ridgeway 1907-2007 A History of The Christian and Missionary Alliance Church of White Plains*, Createspace, 2008. Print.

Mr. Mako is available to consult with you in the following areas of expertise:

-To write or assist in writing the history of your organization.

-Create or assist in creating the archive of your organization.

To contact Richard E. Mako:

e-Mail   Richardemako@Gmail.com

Telephone   914-980-5606

Richard E. Mako, Jr.
©REMarkable Publications, Inc.